OUTLAW SPRINTS

Mike O'Leary

MBI Publishing Company

ACKNOWLEDGEMENTS

In any endeavor such as this, many individuals provide invaluable help in pulling together the right images, accurate information, and hard-to-find data. For their timely assistance, I would like to thank the following:.

- Photographers Randy Jones, John Mahoney, Jack Kromer, E. A. Boase, Jeff Jones, and Linda Jones
- Tom Schmeh, the National Sprint Car Hall of Fame Museum
- Allan E. Brown, *The History of America's Speedways*
- Marc Dailey, Stealth Motorsports
- Steve Hendrickson
- Peter Bodensteiner at MBI
- Bill Klingbeil

First published in 2002 by MBI Publishing Company, Galtier Plaza, Suite 200, 380 Jackson Street, St. Paul, MN 55101-3885 USA

MBI Publishing Company books are also available at discounts in bulk quantity for industrial or sales-promotional use. For details write to Special Sales Manager at Motorbooks International Wholesalers & Distributors, Galtier Plaza, Suite 200, 380 Jackson Street, St. Paul, MN 55101-3885 USA.

Library of Congress Cataloging-in-Publication Data Available
ISBN 0-7603-1156-0

On the front cover: In 2001, Fred Rahmer earned his fifth consecutive Lincoln Speedway championship. *Jeff Jones*

On the frontispiece: Dale Blaney at Devil's Bowl. *Randy Jones*

On the title page: Thunder reverberates through the Pennsylvania mountains, as sprinters charge into the first turn at Williams Grove. When built in 1939, the Grove was modeled after California's legendary Legion Ascot Speedway. *Jack Kromer*

On the back cover:
Top: Steve Kinser gets on the gas quickly at Indiana's Tri-State Speedway. *Randy Jones* **Bottom**: Known as The Preacher, charismatic Jan Opperman waits for the main event to line up at Eldora Speedway in 1976, posing with "Speedy Bill" Smith's Speedway Motors sprinter. *John Mahoney*

Edited by Peter Bodensteiner
Designed by Katie Sonmor

Printed in China

CONTENTS

SPRINT CARS AND OUTLAWS

For pure speed and excitement, it is hard to beat 800-horsepower, mud-slinging sprint cars. As colorful as they are loud, they slide wheel-to-wheel through the turns, rocket quickly down the straightaway and into the next turn, running laps on a dirt track quicker than any other type of racing car.

The men who steer these machines are unique in today's motorsports environment. They are highly talented athletes, fearless and smart, with superior reflexes and eye-hand coordination. By necessity, most are skilled mechanics who have also become part businessman and part public relations expert. And they will still crisscross the country to race several times every weekend, because that is what it takes to put beans on the table and to pay the mortgage.

Three wide at Eldora. Donnie Mack (4, closest), Lee Osborne (81), and Jac Haudenschild (27). *John Mahoney*

The One-Armed Bandit, Chuck Amati, is on the gas at Columbus Speedway in Indiana. The Bruce Cogle Ford-sponsored sprint car was a typical design for the early 1970s. *John Mahoney*

They continue a tradition that began when men wore starched shirts, suits, and bowlers, and the ladies wore dresses and carried parasols. Families have attended races together for generations, and today's race tracks are filled with the descendants of these first spectators. Many of the mothers and fathers in the grandstands at local speedways and in the infield at county fairgrounds watched their first races with their parents and grandparents.

SPRINT CAR RACING'S ROOTS

Sprint car racing has its roots in the earliest days of the passenger car in America. Managers of horse tracks, including those at many popular fairgrounds, found that early automobile speed exhibitions and races were surprisingly popular. Early in the twentieth century, the growing American Automobile Association (AAA, or the "Triple-A") began organizing competitions at these venues. As an example of their popularity, an amazing 36,000 spectators attended one 1906 AAA event in Louisville, Kentucky. One of the early stars was the immortal Barney Oldfield, who barnstormed around the country with his Peerless *Green Dragon*.

By 1915, in the face of continuously increasing fees by AAA, several state fairground managers

Dick Gaines and Karl Kinser formed the only team to win both the Knoxville Nationals and the Little 500. Here, Gaines lifts the left front wheel of Karl Kinser's sprint car at Kokomo Speedway. *John Mahoney*

Hailing from Kansas City Kenny Weld could do it all. He set a record of 40 feature wins and claimed the Knoxville Nationals in the Weikert's Livestock machine in 1973. This photo, taken a year later, is from Williams Grove Speedway. *John Mahoney*

Three outlaw racers share a laugh before hot laps. Rick Ferkel, Shane Carson, and Steve Kinser have won a lot of races between them. *John Mahoney*

Jim Linder's *X* leads Steve Kinser at Eldora. It is easy to spot the different strategies in the evolving design of wings. *John Mahoney*

formed the International Motor Contest Association (IMCA). For the next half-century, the great majority of oval track races were sanctioned by one of these two groups. In a predominantly rural society, 35 state fairground tracks held auto races before World War I, and 7 more took up racing in the years following the war. State fairgrounds held big races each summer, and as the sport flourished, many smaller, local tracks were built for weekly racing.

The cars that competed at Indianapolis ran a national championship schedule, but economics and the interests of safety drove both AAA and IMCA to develop divisions of less powerful cars. In 1933, AAA established a limit of 205 cubic inches for engine displacement in all nonchampionship point events on the Pacific Coast, and this was extended nationwide in 1941. While these cars, known as "big" or "championship" cars, remained the premier racing division, a formula of miniature racing machines, called midgets, was rapidly gaining popularity in many areas of the country.

In the mid-1950s, a new class of racing car evolved that filled the gap between the championship cars and the midgets. They were high powered, lightweight, and economical. They ran races of short duration, often labeled as "sprints" in advertising. In 1956, the United States Auto Club (USAC) had replaced AAA as a national sanctioning organization, and both USAC and IMCA described this class of racing as "sprint cars."

SPRINT CARS GROW WINGS

At the same time, local dirt tracks were employing a variety of styles of machinery, much of it home-made and ungoverned by technical specifications. In many areas, a class of cars called super-modifieds sprang up. The super-modifieds were similar in size and style to sprint cars, but with lightweight roofs that were a holdover from jalopies and stock cars. When roll cages were first developed for sprint cars, they were primarily for safety, but they also allowed sprint car drivers to compete in super-modified races.

Jimmy Boyd (21) is chased by Doug Wolfgang (4x) as he wins the first World of Outlaws race at Devil's Bowl Speedway, Mesquite, Texas, March 18, 1978. *John Mahoney*

The Ohio Traveler, Rick Ferkel, poses with Ted Johnson after winning the World of Outlaws feature at Eldora Speedway. Ferkel nearly captured the first World of Outlaws title. *John Mahoney*

Jim Cushman is credited with racing the first aerodynamic wing, in 1958 at Ohio's Columbus Motor Speedway. An inverted airfoil, the wing used the air rushing over the moving car to create downforce, pushing the vehicle down onto the track and allowing it to corner quicker. Other racers soon copied the device. Sprint cars began adding wings on top of the roll cages, and they grew quickly in popularity.

Tom Schmeh, curator of the National Sprint Car Hall of Fame Museum, says today's sprint car design is a hybrid. "You had super-modifieds running on tracks that were specially built for racing. Then you had the fairgrounds horse tracks, where the big cars were running. I think the modern winged sprint car evolved from both of those. You started seeing them kind of merge together where guys were running basically the same car and just changing the tails or putting a bolt-on cage on as needed to run both series."

THE PENNSYLVANIA POSSE

Sprint car racing has prospered in Pennsylvania. In the early days, the cars were called bugs and Ray Tilley was called a genius. The era of the unforgettable Kenny Weld and Jan Opperman battles set the table for the birth of the Pennsylvania Posse. Whenever any racing series ventured into Pennsylvania, they had to face top Keystone State drivers, and they frequently left with their tails between their legs.

Lynn Schaeffer, who documents the Pennsylvania racing scene with his *Thunder in the Pennsylvania Mountains* and *The Good Ole Daze* video series, remembers, "By 1970, we were paying $600 to win. That doesn't sound like much, but other tracks in the country were paying $150, from what I understand. When you'd go to Williams Grove in 1969, 1970, and 1971, you'd see Kenny Weld from Kansas City, Jan Opperman from California, Sonny Howard from Tennessee, and Bobby Allen and Steve Smith from Florida. Everyone who wanted to make a living running sprint cars had to come around here. Not only did they pay $600 to win, but they paid well above the other tracks all the way through. The top cars from Pennsylvania, like Smokey Snellbaker and Lynn Paxton, could usually run with the invaders.

"There was a time in the mid-1980s when the promoters couldn't do anything wrong," Schaeffer adds. "They had a race on Thanksgiving—the place was packed. No matter what the tracks did, they were just packed. Everyone had those funky sunglasses and a big gaudy racing T-shirt on, and they'd have a beer cooler between them. They were at every race you had."

Steve Kinser won the first World of Outlaws point title. In this shot, following the final race of the 1978 season, Eldora Speedway owner Earl Baltes crowns Kinser the "King of the Outlaws," as Ted Johnson approves. *John Mahoney*

In addition to the visual differences, the super-modifieds matured under less-restrictive rules and, as Schmeh points out, this led to more exploration in design. "You had the box-tails on the super-modifieds, and you had the tin tops, which evolved into the wings. You saw them first on super-modifieds in southern Ohio. Across the country the super-modifieds were the ones that really experimented with the wings first, because they were a kind of run what you brung class."

SPRINT CARS, RACERS, AND OUTLAWS

In some areas, regional racing organizations helped organize the flourishing racers. Most lasted just a couple of seasons, but others were to have a significant impact on the growth of sprint car racing. The Northern Auto Racing Club (NARC) was founded in

1960, and it continued to organize events in northern California and the Pacific Northwest for more than 40 years. The All Stars Circuit of Champions was originally founded in 1970, and renewed by Bert Emick in the early 1980s.

While USAC was the premier organization from its founding in 1956 through the 1970s, a subculture of sprint car racing with little organization and few rules evolved. In his book, *The History of America's Speedways*, author Allan Brown notes that AAA referred to drivers who raced outside of AAA as "outlaws." Three decades later, USAC continued this practice, and frequently suspended drivers who were caught racing in non-USAC "outlaw" events.

Among the top outlaw racers during the 1960s and 1970s were Jan "The Preacher" Opperman; Missouri's Kenny Weld; Bobby "Scruffy" Allen; Steve Kinser; Sammy Swindell from Memphis; Rick Ferkel, the "Ohio Traveler"; Arizona's Leland McSpadden; Bubby Jones; and Doug "Wolfie" Wolfgang. These racers were able to make a living by competing in as many of these unsanctioned events as possible. They'd finish a race, load the car onto an open trailer, collect their pay, and head to the next track. As often as not, they'd sleep in the back seat of the car or in the pickup truck they towed with. Their route was determined by the next race.

Many top drivers have used sprint cars as a stepping stone. Dave Blaney won the World of Outlaws championship while Al Unser Jr., Tony Stewart, and Kenny Schrader cut their racing teeth in sprinters. Jeff Gordon, caught here at Eldora in 1988, began racing sprint cars when he was 15 years old. *John Mahoney*

As Tom Schmeh points out, this gypsy lifestyle set the pattern for today's sprint car racers. "Picking and choosing the big money races became another identifying mark for the outlaws. They would go into a town, take as much money as they could, and move on."

A big purse would draw many of the best-known outlaws. After promoting several successful events in 1977, Ted Johnson initiated the World of Outlaws. By negotiating better-paying races and appearance fees with a series of tracks, Johnson could guarantee that the top drivers would compete. Jimmy Boyd, driving Kenny Woodruff's sprint car, won the first event on March 18, 1978, at Devil's Bowl Speedway in Dallas. Putting together a schedule with 41 events that stretched from New York to California, Johnson offered the gypsy drivers and crews a more stable season with better profitability. Fans immediately took to the series, filling the grandstands wherever they raced.

The World of Outlaws attracted large crowds during its first year. Here the Outlaws get ready to race in front of packed grandstands and pits. *John Mahoney*

A NIGHT AT THE RACES

Take three or four dozen winged sprint cars, add a purse that provides the biggest payoff of the weekend, and simmer throughout a boiling hot summer afternoon. This is the recipe that attracts sprint car fans around the country.

Sprint car races start and finish at full gallop. The path to the pay window only requires two laps of qualifying, a dozen or so laps in a heat race, and then the main event. All told the cars will complete less than 40 green flag miles, even if the fastest cars run a dash. There is little time for strategy and no pacing for the long run. When you push off, it's time to make it pay.

Frankie Kerr and Steve Kinser wait for qualifying at Terre Haute. *Randy Jones*

Preparing the track before racing starts at
Tri-State Speedway. *Randy Jones*

BEFORE THE GREEN FLAG

Motor homes pull into the track's parking lot
early, and a small village begins to grow. Chairs and
tables are set up and awnings are raised. Soon, char-
coal grills are filling the air with tangy smells, from
hot dogs to T-bones. Fans begin invading the track's
grandstands and hillsides hours before the first green
flag. They stake out their territory with lawn chairs
and blankets. They have coolers, newspapers, and
programs, and they start up conversations with their
neighbors that will last hours into the night.

Late in the afternoon, the big racing rigs begin
rolling through the pit gate. They are brightly colored
and parked side-by-side, six feet apart, with their
chrome taillights in a row. Every member of every

Big rigs crossing the track at Eldora.
Randy Jones

crew knows what needs to be done. While teams perform their tasks in slightly different manners, they all have the same job—getting ready to race.

As they come into the track, the driver or the crew chief will stop at the officials' table and draw a number from a bag or raffle wheel. This determines the order of the qualifying line-up and can have a big impact on how the night is going to go. Within each team, the assignment goes to whoever develops the reputation for drawing the best numbers.

The tailgate is lowered and the crew begins setting up shop. The car is rolled out. Then a 5-foot high toolbox is rolled down the incline, and stacks of tires are unloaded. The wing is brought out and

Steve Kinser takes time to sign autographs before suiting up. *Randy Jones*

The crews are busy making final adjustments as they ready the cars to go on the track. *Randy Jones*

One of the many types of four-wheelers used in the pits. This workaholic is affectionately called a "mule."
Randy Jones

mounted on top of the car. One crewman begins spraying an oily lubricant onto every exposed section of the car's body and frame (some even use plain baby oil). Later, this will help them scrape the mud and clay off the machine.

While the crewmen are busy, the driver and crew chief begin evaluating the conditions. "We try to take a look at what the shape of the track is," says Donny Schatz, a top racer on the World of Outlaws circuit. "We normally get there at four o'clock at the latest, and normally don't get on the track until six or six-thirty. We try to determine at what point we're going to start off with the race car, shocks, tires, all of those things. It's not so much focusing on the shape of the track, it's more the conditioning and what we think it's going to do. We also look at the weather, to see how good the air is, so we can tune the engine. There are quite a few things that we look into when we first get there."

A four-wheeled utility vehicle, often called a "mule," is rolled out of the trailer. Mules, in all their different designs and configurations, perform the same functions, pushing the car around the pit area and carrying spare parts. If the crew has the opportunity to work on the car during a race, the mule will have nearly everything it needs. The mule can carry a variety of shocks, spacers, a front axle, an air compressor, a rear end, electrical cables, a vise for quickly straightening bent parts, several plastic fuel cans, and a variety of tools. Some even have a platform on top that a mechanic can stand on to watch the race.

When the drivers' meeting is called, a variety of people respond, including track workers, car owners, and media representatives. While content of the meetings varies widely, officials usually discuss the program planned for the event, perhaps clarify or emphasize a rule or a procedure, make necessary announcements, and generally make sure that drivers new to the track know what to expect.

The drivers' meeting attracts officials, team members, the press, and others. *Randy Jones*

Warming the engines is critical prior to going out on the track. After being push-started, these cars will drive back to their pit to allow the motor to warm before hot lapping. *Randy Jones*

HOT LAPS

As the time for hot laps approaches, drivers will get into their cars and be pushed just to start the engine, and then the car will be brought back to the pit area and allowed to idle. Schatz explains, "It's strictly to get heat in the engine. With as much compression as they have, and as close as all of the tolerances are, they have to have heat in them all the time. We fire them up to get heat in the car, make sure there are no leaks, make sure that everything is hitting on all eight cylinders, and there's nothing broke. As hard as race engines run, they could develop a problem even when not racing. It's good to get them fired plenty early and make sure that they don't have a problem."

Soon groups of cars are pushed off for hot laps, with the earliest qualifiers in the first group. After a couple of slow laps while all of the cars are started, the drivers are given the green flag. The flagman makes sure that each group gets the same number of laps, usually only three to five, to minimize the wear on the track.

"The first thing that I do when I push off is try to get an open race track," says Schatz. "Hot laps are about the only time of the night that you're not going to get penalized for the way you're performing. You have to know what your race car is doing and you only get two laps to do it. Most places you'll get a guy who wants to drive in front of you and try to race. But hot laps are not anything about racing. It's all about trying to find a happy medium for your race car and make sure everything's running. So that's virtually the only time you get on the track before qualifying."

Kenny Jacobs, a four-time champion with the All Stars, agrees. "I try to run at least one or two laps real fast to see if the car feels the way I want it to feel. Hot laps tell me a lot of how my whole night's going to go. I really concentrate in hot laps, because qualifying means so much, and I think hot laps mean a lot more than they used to. I try to make sure our car's really fast for hot laps so that we'll know what it will do for qualifying."

Most crew chiefs have a good set of notes for nearly every track they will race on. This allows them

Jeff Swindell, the younger brother of Sammy, qualifies at Canyon Speedway. *Randy Jones*

James and P.J. Chesson are among the young guns in sprint car racing. Here James is on a qualifying lap at the Terre Haute Action Track. *Randy Jones*

to accurately prepare the car before they get to the track. Jacobs notes that it has become easier. "We run the same (torsion) bar and shock combination at 90 percent of the tracks we go to with these new cars, . Very rarely do we change a bar anymore. We just change shocks and tire stagger combinations, and move the wing around a little bit, and race the car."

AERODYNAMICS AND TRACTION

The team's adjustments focus on finding the optimum balance for the car and the conditions; variables include the track, the conditions that night, and the driver's preferences.

As with most other forms of racing, aerodynamics have become critical to winged sprint cars. In sprint cars, it isn't a matter of making the car clean and smooth to reduce aero drag. It's more important to use the air to make the machine handle properly. The 25-square-foot wing is literally an inverted airfoil that presses the rear tires onto the track. As the car goes into the turn and the driver turns to the left, the back end of the car tends to slide out, but the sideboards on the wing catch the air and quickly put more pressure on the left rear wheel. The result is a feeling that the car is "planted," and the driver can go through the turn much faster than without the wing. The small front wing performs a simple function. While so much energy is focused on the rear of the car, the front wing works to keep the front wheels in contact with the track so the driver can steer.

The driver can adjust the top wing from inside the car, applying a hydraulic control to slide it forward

Jimmy Carr at Bloomington Speedway. Canadian Carr has won the Knoxville Nationals twice and the World of Outlaws title as Danny Lasoski's crew chief. *Randy Jones*

Kevin Gobrecht had a bright future before his untimely death just weeks after winning the 1999 Historical Big One. Here he is qualifying at Haubstadt's Tri-State Speedway. *Randy Jones*

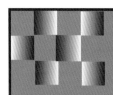

ROLL CAGE PADDING

Kenny Jacobs says that some of the most overlooked safety items in a sprint car are the foam pads fastened to the top and sides of the roll cage. "I think that the window nets and the arm restraints, the wrap -around high-backed seats, the new frame side rails, and the kick- out rails, all of that is really good. The padding on the roll cage that the All Stars make mandatory, I think is a great thing. I've been knocked out three times and it takes longer to get over than getting beat up. When you get the crap beat out of you in a crash but don't ding your head, you can withstand it and race the next night, no problem. If you ding your head and come back the next night, everything's going faster than you are. I think roll cage padding is a great thing, and it should be mandatory in all sprint cars because it weighs absolutely nothing and it's a great safety factor."

and back in a track. As it rolls back, the rear of the wing is also pushed up, increasing the wing's angle. With the wing in the rear position, the driver will put more downforce on the rear wheels. The trade-off is an increase in aerodynamic drag. As the wing moves forward, downforce is taken out. The car will be faster on the straights, but have less grip in the turns. On starts, having the wing in the rear position will give the car more traction as the driver accelerates.

Tire stagger is the difference in circumference between the left rear tire and the larger right rear tire. It isn't unusual to run with a difference of 14 inches between the tires. Increasing stagger helps the car turn, while reducing the stagger will help it run better in a straight line. If the car is pushing, or trying to drive straight ahead while the driver is turning the wheel, additional stagger will help it turn. If the back end of the car feels as if it is going to spin out whenever the driver is in the turn, reducing the stagger will make it more stable and allow the driver to accelerate more.

As with any racing machine, the tire's contact patches are the only four places a sprint car touches the racing surface. Modern sprint car tires are available in several compounds, generally ranging from

On the hook. A sprint car being moved back to the pits after wrecking at Eldora. *Randy Jones*

soft to hard. It is a simple equation; the softer tire generally grips the track better but wears out quicker. As the tire wears out, it can lose its tread and its grip, it can blister and ride very rough, or it can blow and cause the car to wreck. The driver and crew have to decide which tire compound to use before each race. It takes a lot of experience to accurately predict how a track will change during the course of a race. Will it become dry and hard? Will a softer tire remain competitive near the end of the race?

Jacobs describes his approach at some tracks. "We run more pressure in the left rear tire on the big fast tracks, so the car can't bury the left rear tire into the track and wrinkle the tire so bad when it enters the corner. Because of the offset wing sideboard stagger, the side pressure of the wing when you start to enter the corner on a real high-speed track is trying to bury the inside of the car. So we run a little more air pressure in the left rear tire. It helps hold that corner up, so it doesn't get into the race track."

One element of the witchcraft that top mechanics employ is called "siping" or "grooving." A specially designed, knife-like "siping tool" is used to carve grooves in the tire's tread. The primary purpose of siping tires is to help them last longer. The grooves allow the rubber to dissipate heat so the tire will run longer without getting too hot. Siping techniques vary according to the tires, the track, and the crew chief.

Other settings and adjustments help fine-tune the car for the track and conditions. Torsion bars and shocks control the way the car rides and its reaction to the motion of the wheels over the track. Each corner of the car can be adjusted independently to give more travel, or to stiffen or loosen the car's handling. The driver must make numerous decisions to match the car to the track. (Is he running low or high on the cushion? Is the track tacky or dry? Are there long straightaways? Are the turns banked? Does he need more or less grip?) He will want the car to perform certain a certain way, and will tune the shocks and torsion bars to adjust the car's handling.

While the racing continues on the track, crews are busy behind the scenes. *Randy Jones*

QUALIFYING

Qualifying demands the two absolutely fastest circuits the driver can run around the oval. After only a handful of hot laps, he has to pull his seat belts tight and hold on while he stands on the gas. In a very short time, he has to decide which groove is going to be fastest while he is on the track and then turn very precise lines.

Crews swarm over the cars between races. Danny Smith's crew is busy during an All Stars event at Bloomington, Indiana. *E. A. Boase*

Different organizations and tracks use various approaches to establish the line-up for the main event. Qualifying times are normally used to determine the heat race line-ups. The fastest six or eight cars in each heat are inverted and will have to race past the slower cars to transfer to the feature. In some organizations, heat race winners will run a race to determine the starting line-up for the main event. In others, the six fastest qualifiers who have made the transfer are inverted for the main. The cars that don't transfer from the heat races will run a semi-main for the final couple of starting spots.

For several decades, Pennsylvania tracks have used a unique but effective method of conducting

Experienced track officials keep the racing program moving smoothly. Eldora's owner, Earl Baltes, coordinates with one of his pit stewards. *Randy Jones*

races, aside from events involving touring groups. Instead of time trials, each track awards points based on prize money earned during the season. Cars qualify for feature races through heat race finishes and are lined up with the top 12 in points inverted. Thus, the highest-ranking car will start outside the sixth row. Pennsylvanians love to argue that this approach provides superior racing, because more cars have an opportunity to win and the best drivers always have to work harder.

DIRT TRACK TECHNIQUES

It doesn't matter how the line-up is determined, sprint car racing is demanding on both drivers and machines. Donny Schatz explains that he has learned not to employ any specific strategy. "I just expect to react to what's happening. I've got seven hundred and some starts with the Outlaws, and after that period of time you just learn to react to what happens and try to make the decisions that you need to make."

The technique of driving a winged sprinter is different from many other popular forms of motorsports. One rule of racing physics states that the straighter the front wheels are, the faster you're going to go, but this doesn't always work on a dirt track. A sprint car thrives on momentum. The more momentum the driver can maintain around the track, the quicker he'll be. But when he is racing another car, under some conditions quick acceleration may pay more dividends than momentum.

As a racing program progresses, the cars will toss the track clay to the outside of the track. Eventually the clay will build up on the outside of the top groove and form a lip, or cushion, that the driver can lean his right rear tire against as he goes through the turn. Generally, this will give him a little more grip and allow him to carry more momentum through the turns.

At the same time, the inside groove is always the shorter way around the track. Even though a driver may sacrifice some momentum by running the "bottom" groove, if his huge rear tires get good grip as the car comes off the turn, the acceleration of 800 horsepower can compensate for having less momentum.

Other factors can come into play. As a car speeds through a corner, tremendous energy pushes the car toward the wall, just as the driver is trying to turn it onto the straightaway. He can't begin to accelerate until the wheels get a good bite, or he'll spin the tires or slide into the wall. Most of the time, the driver who can accelerate first as they come off the turns is the one who will pull ahead.

Good drivers quickly learn that they have to focus on more than the cars they're competing against. They have to watch the track and try to understand where it is the fastest. They can learn a lot by watching the other cars. And as the racing goes on, the track conditions will change. What is fast now may be a lot slower in five laps.

Drivers learn to look for shiny spots on the track. As the tires from more than 20 cars circle, tossing clay toward the top of the groove, some parts of the track will begin to get smooth. As more cars pass over the surface, their tires will begin to slip and spin. The track will become very shiny, almost as if

Donny Schatz takes time to focus before climbing into his car for the main event at the King's Royal. *Randy Jones*

it were being polished each lap. The drivers will quickly adjust their lines to avoid running into the slick spots with their rear tires.

Although it may sound obvious, good visibility is critical to a sprint car driver. The drivers attach several tearoffs—thin sheets of clear plastic—on their helmet visors. As soon as the top one gets covered with mud, the driver can discard it

Oval track racing isn't just about going fast. A rule for the successful driver is to be able to drive where the other cars aren't, so he'll be able to pass. Dave Darland and Mike Mann battle during an All Stars event at Paragon. *Randy Jones*

with one hand and have several more clear ones underneath, temporarily restoring his ability to see. A light rain or mist may not make the track too slippery to race on, but mud from the track, caked and streaked on the driver's visor, and the glare of the bright lights can reduce visibility and make it unsafe to race.

Cement walls surround many sprint car tracks. At some tracks the dirt thrown up by the cars will blanket the walls, making them difficult to see from inside a speeding race car. Between races, the track's crew will scrape diagonal stripes of mud from the walls with shovels, giving the drivers a better view of the turn.

SAFETY FIRST

Sprint cars, evolving in an environment of high-speed, wheel-to-wheel racing, have become safer

Jim Moulis rides out a spectacular flip at Eldora. *Randy Jones*

Steve Kinser has won the Historical Big One more often than any other driver. But winning never gets old. *Randy Jones*

Kelly Kinser runs a competitive car on a limited budget. With a $10,000 payday, he enjoys victory lane ceremonies following his triumph in Lawrenceburg Speedway's Hoosier Fall Classic. *Randy Jones*

every year. While the chassis and bolt-on equipment has become lighter, it has also become better able to absorb energy during a wreck. The wing on top of a sprint car will act in several ways to minimize the violence of an accident. The large flat areas will catch air and help disperse the energy that is causing a car to tumble, and when the car lands on the wing, it dissipates much of the energy that would otherwise be transferred to the car and driver.

The motion of the driver's head in an accident has been the focus of much publicity. Recent developments have included the Head and Neck Restraint System (HANS) and other similar devices that tether the helmet to prevent violent whiplash. For years, other helmet and neck restraints, like the "horse collar," have been effectively used to prevent neck injuries to drivers.

The sprint car community has been aware of the dangers of racing for many years, and improvements to the cars have been continuous. More side and top bars have been designed into the chassis during construction, and builders have added bars to prevent the wheel of another car from making contact with the driver during an accident. An added benefit of the additional bars is that they strengthen the overall integrity of the roll cage. Window nets keep the driver's helmet from going outside the roll cage during a wreck, and restraints keep the driver's arms inside the cage in a tumble.

Track and organization officials periodically inspect sprint cars, particularly those that aren't regular competitors with them, to make sure that each car is within their rules, has the required safety equipment, and that seat belts aren't worn out or obsolete. Additionally some organizations and tracks ban certain lightweight parts, and others require special racing mufflers to reduce noise.

GOING FOR THE CHECKERS

Most drivers agree that except on rare occasions, sprint car racing has little room for strategy. Jacobs says that even though he may think about what he is going to do, it only works part of the time.

"In my own mind, I think about what I'm going to do the first couple of laps," he explained. "And I think of that according to who's in front of me. That's because I've raced against most of the guys in the whole country at one time or another. If I start behind somebody, I usually know how he is going to approach the first corner and, in my mind, I tell myself what I'm going to do. But half the time that doesn't work out, and I do something else anyhow. But I think for most guys, it's just running through their mind what's going to happen in that first corner, and you determine that by who starts in front of you."

One of the conditions that drivers have to anticipate is the groove beginning to develop a build-up of rubber. "It gets tremendous grip," Jacobs explains. "We actually prepare our race car for the rubber the way we would if we were on a real sticky race track. They're very similar setups."

Schatz points out, "When a track takes rubber, it's generally a bad thing. It gets so hard and so abrasive that it actually feels as if you were racing on asphalt. It would feel like turning a corner on your street car. It squeals, it squawks, it's locked down, it's just like taking your street car out and driving it on an asphalt track. It wears the tires very badly. When you slide out of the rubber, it would be like sliding from out of the street onto a frozen lake. You slide out of it and you can get freight-trained by 10 or 12 guys and not ever get back by any of them."

Sprint car racing is all about winning races. There are no style points. At the checkered flag, the winner celebrates in victory lane while the other crews load their cars and equipment. Soon the winning team will return to its trailer. Competitors stop and offer congratulations with a slap on the back or handshake. As one of the last haulers to roll out of the pits, the winner's celebration has been short. They almost immediately begin planning for the next race.

THE RACERS

The people who have chosen the life of sprint car racing are a diverse group with all sorts of backgrounds and accomplishments. While the careers of some are rapidly climbing, others have been around the block and are now enjoying life as senior members of the racing fraternity. Wherever sprint car racers convene, the pits are filled with a colorful assortment of characters.

STEVE KINSER

Sprint car racers will always be measured against Indiana's Kinser family. When it comes to driving, owning, preparing the cars, or making a new innovation work, someone named Kinser has always been among of the very best.

Kenny Jacobs, one of the few drivers who owns his own sprint car team, has more wins than anyone in the All Stars Circuit of Champions. *Randy Jones*

Steve Kinser was in his first year driving for his Uncle Karl, and Doug Wolfgang was one of the top Outlaw racers in the country. This postrace conversation is at Kokomo Speedway in 1978. *John Mahoney*

Steve Kinser is known as the King of the Outlaws. Since his first race in a sprint car in 1976, Steve has compiled so many wins in the World of Outlaws (451 "A" feature victories) and championships (16), that no one else is even statistically close. Steve drove for his Uncle Karl for 16 years, then earned two titles driving cars that he owned. The most prolific Outlaw, his record in big money races is unparalleled. He has won the Knoxville Nationals 11 times. Add 9 Gold Cup titles, the

Williams Grove Open 3 times, the King's Royal, and the Historical Big One.

While in high school, Steve was a champion wrestler in Bloomington, Indiana. His father, Bob Kinser, was one of the toughest racers of the time. Steve and his brother, Randy, were at the local tracks every week with their father, and it was natural for them to aspire to become sprint car drivers. By 1976, both boys were racing, and in 1977, Steve's second full season, he won the South Central Indiana Racing Association championship, driving for Jerry Shields. One of the hottest sprint car teams in Midwest in the 1970s was based just down the highway from Bloomington. It was run by Bob's cousin, Karl Kinser, and featured Dick Gaines behind the wheel. When Gaines was seriously injured late in the fall of 1977, Karl Kinser hired Steve to drive. As 1978 began, they won their first nine races together. That was also the year the World of Outlaws started, and together, Steve and Karl claimed 11 feature races and the first Outlaw championship.

For 16 years, Karl and Steve were nearly unbeatable, winning the World of Outlaws championship every year but two, and averaging 22.5 Outlaws "A" feature wins each season. Then in 1995, Steve took

Three generations of racers. Bob Kinser raced sprint cars into his 60s and is already in the Hall of Fame. While his son, Steve, is sure to follow, Steve's son, Kraig, is just embarking on a sprint car career and may join both of them in the Hall. *Linda Jones*

A panel of Sprint Car Hall of Fame voters named Steve Kinser, with nearly 450 victories, the greatest sprint car driver in history. Steve has competed in the Indianapolis 500 and had a short stint in NASCAR's Winston Cup series. Proving to be a quick study, he won a thrilling IROC (International Race of Champions) race at Talladega. *Randy Jones*

advantage of an opportunity to race in NASCAR's Winston Cup series and left the sprint car trail.

With year-old equipment and little testing, Steve was facing an uphill battle, and after four months with mixed results, he quit NASCAR and returned to Indiana. Since Karl was re-forming his team around his son, Mark, Steve started building a new sprint car team from scratch. Picking up midway into the summer, Steve's Quaker State car won an amazing 18 races and finished ninth in points.

In 1998, Steve claimed six "A" mains and five preliminary features, and earned his 15th World of Outlaws championship. Winning it with his own team brought him special satisfaction. Proving 1998 was no fluke, Steve also earned the 2000 Outlaws title.

KARL AND MARK KINSER

Not 20 miles south of Steve Kinser's Bloomington-based operation is the shop of his uncle, Karl. For 30 years, Karl Kinser has been the definition of a sprint car Outlaw. Championship

From 1995 through 2001, Karl and Mark Kinser, from Oolitic, Indiana, have won nearly twice as many World of Outlaw races as anyone else. *Randy Jones*

trophies mean little. With his focus set on prize money, Karl has been able to make his living by running a sprint car, and no one else has done it for as long. For many years, Karl was not only the car owner and chief mechanic, but he also designed and built his own chassis and engines.

Karl Kinser's sprint cars have won every big money race at every big race track in the country. Karl has stood in victory lane at the Knoxville Nationals 12 times, 9 with Steve and 3 with his son, Mark. He's won the King's Royal, the Williams Grove National Open, the Historical Big One, the Gold Cup, and the Western World. His teams have earned 17 World of Outlaws championship trophies.

While Karl and Steve were dominating the top rung of sprint car racing, Mark was learning the ropes with his own team. When Steve left the team, it was natural for Karl and Mark to join forces. They soon began visiting victory lane on a regular basis.

After winning the Williams Grove National Open and the U.S. Dirt Nationals in 1995, Mark and Karl put it all together the next year, collecting the Knoxville Nationals on their way to the Outlaws championship. In 1997, Mark seized an opportunity to race with an upstart NASCAR truck team and missed several World of Outlaws events. It didn't slow Karl, as he employed several drivers, including Mark's cousin, Kelly Kinser, and once again topped the Outlaws car owners' points.

Virtually every decision Karl makes centers around putting food on the table and tires on the sprint car. His innovations were designed to win money. After trailing Steve Kinser in the 1998 Outlaw championship, Karl and Mark made a bold move. After decades of running Chevys, they switched motors. Chrysler had been attempting to break into sprint car racing with their Mopar brand for several years, and made Karl a lucrative offer. With Gary Stanton building the engines and the Mopar penta-star emblazoned on the car, they attacked the 1999 season. After a hard-fought battle with Danny Lasoski and Steve, they notched 19

With a Knoxville Nationals victory and an Outlaws championship, Mark Kinser put Mopar's alternative sprint car engine on the map. *Randy Jones*

race wins, bagged their second Knoxville Nationals victory, and earned another World of Outlaws title.

Mark appears to be on his way to writing his own chapter in World of Outlaws history. In the seven years since teaming with his father, he has won the most World of Outlaws feature races in every year but two, and nearly twice as many (124) as anyone else. In 2001, Kinser again scored the most victories, adding his first King's Royal and Gold Cup Race of Champions victories.

SAMMY SWINDELL

The son of a hard-nosed racer, Sammy Swindell grew up at race tracks around his Memphis home. As

An outlaw before the Outlaws, Sammy Swindell ran well in Indy cars for A. J. Foyt and Pat Patrick, as well as in the Busch series, and in NASCAR trucks. He won the Chili Bowl midget event four times. But he always came back to the sprinters. *Randy Jones*

Andy Hillenburg, from Broken Arrow, Oklahoma, has been a mainstay of the Outlaws tour for more than a decade. He's another driver who has been successful with his own racing team. *Randy Jones*

a teenager, he excelled in the three racing divisions at Riverside Speedway in West Memphis. While still in high school, Sammy began expanding his horizon, taking his car across the Mississippi to tracks in Missouri, and he became a regular at Devil's Bowl in Mesquite, Texas. When the World of Outlaws was formed in 1978, Swindell won two features during the inaugural season.

While the Kinsers appear to have dominated the World of Outlaws record book, they had to go through Swindell to get there. The wheel-to-wheel battles between Sammy and Steve are legendary. For the first decade of the World of Outlaws, Sammy was the only driver to take the championship from Steve and Karl. Driving LaVerne Nance's renowned sprint car, and doing his own tuning and maintenance, he won the titles in 1981 and 1982.

By the mid-1980s, Swindell began looking beyond sprint car racing. He performed flawlessly in Indy car opportunities with Pat Patrick and A. J. Foyt, but was never able to put together a consistent ride. In 1987, he tried Indy in a year-old car with a stock-block Pontiac, but was the last car bumped from the starting field. Continuing to look outside sprint cars, he ran part of one season with NASCAR's Busch Grand National circuit, and another in the Craftsman Truck Series. But he always returned to sprint cars.

Sammy is the second-winningest driver in the history of the World of Outlaws, and in 1997 earned his third championship. This time he was driving his own car, the powder blue Number 1 Channellock machine. In 2000, he began to cut back on his racing efforts in order to devote more time to his family and his son's budding racing career. In mid-2001, Swindell suffered severe injuries while qualifying at Lernerville, when a push truck pulled onto the track in front of him. Although he returned to the cockpit, he has continued to pursue a reduced schedule.

DANNY LASOSKI

When Danny "The Dude" Lasoski won the 2001 World of Outlaws championship, it capped a quest that began at Saline County Speedway in Marshall, Missouri. Lasoski paid his dues, racing as often as he could, putting a lot of miles on his odometer and driving for a variety of teams. Before joining the Outlaw tour full-time, he won more races at Knoxville Raceway than any other driver, and he continues to hold the record with 77 wins and 7 track championships.

For three years, Lasoski chased the Outlaws title, finishing in the top five in points each year. Driving Dennis Roth's Beef Packers sprinter, he achieved one of his dreams when he won the 1998 Knoxville Nationals after a memorable battle with Sammy Swindell.

Everything finally came together when Tony Stewart decided to build a sprint car team around his friend for the 2001 racing season. Relying on consistency throughout a season-long battle with Mark Kinser, Lasoski claimed the point crown. On the way, he earned his second Knoxville Nationals victory.

Danny Lasoski had a full career before being hired by Tony Stewart. In his first year driving for Stewart, the Dude was victorious in the Knoxville Nationals and earned the World of Outlaws championship. *Randy Jones*

KENNY JACOBS

Kenny Jacobs, from Holmesville, Ohio, affectionately known as "The Mouse," has been a threat wherever he has raced. He grew up at Lakeside Speedway, battling the Haudenschild brothers, Ed and Jac, and Brad Doty. In 1986, he earned the Rookie-of-the-Year Awards in USAC's Silver Crown and sprint car divisions.

After building his resume on the tough Ohio and Pennsylvania ovals, Jacobs was hired to race the full Outlaw circuit. In three years with Dan and

Putting together his own sprint car team out of necessity, Kenny Jacobs won two All Star championships and became the winningest driver in the history of that series. *Randy Jones*

Tom Motter's Ecowater sprint car, he finished sixth, fourth, and seventh in points. The Mouse scored the biggest victory of his racing career in 1994, when he took home all the marbles at the second running of the $100,000 Historical Big One at Eldora.

Returning to Ohio in 1998, he joined the All Stars Circuit of Champions tour and won the championship. The next season he started his own racing team and won three consecutive titles. Jacobs is the winningest driver in the history of the All Stars with 95 feature victories, nearly double the total of anyone else.

DONNY SCHATZ

Since the Dakotas are better known for bull riders, it seems appropriate that when a Dakotan sprint car driver heads south to race full-time, he is exceptionally talented. Doug Wolfgang, from Sioux Falls, South Dakota, was one of the first to leave his mark on the Outlaw trail. Now, Donny Schatz from Minot, North Dakota, is following those footsteps.

Schatz recalls, "My parents used to take me to see the Outlaws in Fargo and at the Nationals, and

Donny Schatz is part of the new generation and poised to win a lot of sprint car races. He left Minot, North Dakota, to go on the road with his team. *Randy Jones*

FROM *Brand X* TO THE CHAMPIONSHIP

While Karl and Steve Kinser formed the most successful sprint car duo on the Outlaws trail, Mark Kinser built a successful sprint car career of his own. Initially using an older car from Karl's shop, Mark's car was called *Brand X*. He began traveling with the Outlaws in 1984 and shared the Rookie-of-the-Year Award that season. He was soon hired to drive for other teams. In 1991, driving Ray and Jay Williams' *Payless Maxim*, Mark's three wins and steady finishes earned second in points to his father and Steve.

When Steve left Karl's team to try NASCAR, Karl and Mark quickly merged their teams. After winning the 2001 King's Royal, Mark described the impact of racing for his father. "Before I was running with Dad, I was pretty much getting the swing on my own. I'd win four to seven races a year and I was pretty proud of that. I really thought I knew what was going on. The first year I ran with Dad, we won 24 races, and I didn't make him any better."

it was something that I always had the desire to do. I thought it was the coolest thing on earth, and I still do. It's hard to say what about it motivated me to want to race sprint cars, but it's just something that I've dreamt about since I was five years old."

Donny joined Wissota, a regional sprint car group that races primarily in Wisconsin, Minnesota, and neighboring states. In his first year behind the wheel of a sprint car, he earned the 1993 Wissota Rookie-of-the-Year Award. As he honed his skills, he began running 410 sprints in addition to the 360-ci Wissota cars and facing off with the Outlaws several times each season. In 1996, he earned the Wissota national title with 25 victories. The next season, he went on the road with the Outlaws, and he earned the Rookie-of-the-Year title.

Proving to be one of the best of a new generation of sprint car racers, Schatz joined forces with famed mechanic Kenny Woodruff to head his Parker Stores operation. In 2001, their first full season together, Schatz won 10 times on the Outlaw circuit and finished fifth in points. He added his name to the list of winners of one of the oldest running events in the country, the Williams Grove Open. For the past four years, during the off-season, he has taken his tour down under, winning the Standard Grand Annual Sprintcar Classic back-to-back in 2001 and 2002, and the 2002 Parts Plus Summer Slam at Parramatta City Raceway in Australia.

KENNY WOODRUFF

Kenny Woodruff, originally from Fort Dodge, Iowa, has been a stalwart of the sprint car scene for more than 30 years. When Jimmy Boyd won the first World of Outlaws race in a machine Woodruff owned and prepared, Woodruff's place in sprint car history was secure. The list of drivers who have piloted Woodruff-wrenched sprint cars is impressive, including Outlaws Champions Bobby Davis Jr. (1989) and Dave Blaney (1995). Others Woodruff has worked with include Danny Smith, Doug Wolfgang, Steve Kinser, Sammy and Jeff Swindell, Ron Shuman, Danny Lasoski, Kevin Gobrecht, Dale Blaney, and Daryn Pittman. Kenny has enjoyed victory lane at the Knoxville Nationals (1997), Historical Big One and King's Royal (three times each), the Gold Cup (1997), and Western World Championship (1991).

When he joined Donny Schatz during the Knoxville Nationals in 2000, results came quickly. "The first race out with Kenny was really a big deal," relates Schatz. "We were in a position to win THE race in sprint car racing, but I made some mistakes and we finished second."

Kenny Woodruff is the only crew chief on the trail with experience comparable to Karl Kinser. When Woodruff joined Schatz, their program improved immediately. *Randy Jones*

BRENT KAEDING

When one looks at the records of West Coast sprint car racers, it's easy to see that Brent Kaeding dominates most of them. The Campbell, California, clan includes Brent's father, Howard, and sons Tim and Bud, each a respected sprint car racer. Brent has earned 13 Northern Auto Racing Club (NARC) championships, and claimed the King of California crown 11 times. His career has been varied as he has also earned victories in the Turkey Night midget classic and in the California Racing Association (CRA) and Sprint Car Racing Association (SCRA) non-winged sprint car competition.

JAC HAUDENSCHILD

The "Wild Child" grew up around race tracks in Ohio with his older brother, Ed, who was the first to begin racing. Coming from the same rural area and nearly the same age as Kenny Jacobs and Brad Doty, the three were close friends as they competed against each other at nearby tracks. Growing a legion of fans,

Not only has Brent Kaeding collected 11 King of California crowns and 13 NARC championships, he has also won the Turkey Night midget classic. Here he hustles through a turn at the Las Vegas dirt oval. *Randy Jones*

Before suffering serious injuries at Eldora, Brad Doty was a rapidly rising star with the World of Outlaws. Today, he has become a popular sprint car commentator on television. *Randy Jones*

Jac has been most successful in big money races, winning the inaugural Historical Big One and three King's Royal crowns. Haudenschild captured a pair of Gold Cups and once earned the Hard Charger Award for passing 44 cars during the Saturday night races at the Knoxville Nationals.

THE PENNSYLVANIA POSSE

Many who love sprint car racing consider Pennsylvania the promised land. The racing starts early in the year and continues well into October. Years ago, anyone venturing into the Keystone State to race learned that its weekly circuit was the toughest in the country and the Pennsylvania Posse was hard to catch.

For more than three decades, Mifflintown's Keith Kauffman has been winning sprint car races, and he's

Steve Smith was one of the toughest of the Pennsylvania Posse. When Stevie needed a car for the World of Outlaws tour, the father and son built their own machine. *E. A. Boase*

Lincoln Speedway is one of the homes of the Pennsylvania Posse. Billy Dietrich (8) and Fred Rahmer (77) lead Don Kreitz Jr. (69) and Danny Jones through a turn. *Jack Kromer*

Keith Kauffman has won more than 250 feature races in 30 years with the Pennsylvania Posse. *Jeff Jones*

garnered more than 250 checkered flags. He has had several opportunities to compete in top equipment with the World of Outlaws and the All Stars. Now Kauffman has returned to his Pennsylvania roots, and he remains one of the most successful sprint car drivers in history. In 2001, Kauffman claimed his 10th Port Royal Speedway track championship, 24 years after his first.

Fred Rahmer has developed a love-hate relationship with Pennsylvania fans. When he arrives in victory lane he is usually met with as many boos as cheers. That doesn't bother Rahmer, as long as he is in victory lane. Rahmer has been there a

A true outlaw, through the 1960s and 1970s Kenny Weld became one of the most successful sprint car drivers in history. Following severe personal problems, he emerged to develop the computerized CNC machining process used on racing engines today. *John Mahoney*

lot–more than 250 times. He is second in win totals at both Williams Grove and Lincoln Speedways, and in 2001 he earned his fifth straight Lincoln track championship.

Originally a machinist, Lance Dewease began his racing career in the early 1990s, in cars that he built in his own shop. Today, his feature win total is in the neighborhood of 200, and Dewease has become one of the leaders of the Posse. In 2001, Dewease became the winningest driver in the history of Williams Grove Speedway as he claimed his third track title. He won both the Williams Grove National Open and the Jack Gunn Memorial, the track's biggest races of the year.

ALONG PIT LANE

Danny Smith doesn't look like someone who has been hustling sprint cars around bullrings since 1974. He first garnered a place in racing folklore in 1978, when Karl Kinser chose his nephew Steve over him to replace Dick Gaines in his cars. But a big break came two years later when Smith was hired by C. K. Spurlock to pilot his *Kenny Rogers Special* and earned his first World of Outlaws race victory. During a career spanning more than a quarter-century with the Outlaws and the All Stars, Smith estimates that he has raced for more than 80 different car owners. Twice he's won seven races in

When Karl Kinser needed a driver for the 1978 season, he narrowed his choices to two youngsters, his cousin Steve and Danny Smith. After Karl and Steve hooked up, Smith drove the legendary sprint car sponsored by singer Kenny Rogers. He's been standing on the gas for three decades. *Randy Jones*

one day, but his biggest victory came in the Gold Cup of 1985.

Coming from a family involved in motorsports, Craig Dollansky raced his way out of Minnesota and onto the World of Outlaws tour. After driving for several different owners, Craig put together his own team and subsequently joined forces with Karavan Motorsports. He earned his first Outlaws victory at Perris Auto Speedway in California in 1999. The next season he won the inaugural point championship of the Outlaws Gumout support series. Joining the road full-time with the Outlaws in 2001, Dollansky claimed a pair of wins while putting together a strong effort that led to fourth place in the points.

Brian and Sarah Carlson have been married 14 years. They have also been racing together for 14 years, the past six in sprint cars. While Brian drives, Sarah is one of the few female crew chiefs in sprint car racing. Following several years of competition with the All Stars, the Carlsons competed with the Outlaws' Gumout series in 2000 and 2001. Although they have yet to find victory lane in either of these series, the family from Linden, Indiana, has consistently fielded competitive cars.

Sprint car racing remains strong, as evidenced by the crop of young racers climbing the ladder. They include Brownsburg, Indiana's Joey Saldana, the son of a Hall of Fame sprint car driver and Indianapolis 500 veteran. Joey ranks second in All Stars career victories (59) and has added four Outlaws wins to his resume.

Brian and Sarah Carlson have been able to run a modest but competitive sprint car effort with both the All Stars and the Gumout series. One of the few hands-on female crew chiefs in the sprint car pits, Sarah was obviously pregnant with their first child during the 2001 King's Royal. *Randy Jones*

One of the young lions in sprint cars, Joey Saldana claimed 59 All Stars race victories before joining the Outlaws. Here, he shows that at Indiana's Tri-State Speedway, you sometimes pull both front wheels off the ground getting off turn four quickly. *Randy Jones*

4

GOING RACING

S o you've just won the lottery and have decided to go sprint car racing. Where do you start? What do you need? There are no single answers to these questions. You can put together a sprint car team using a realistic budget, or this sport will devour as much money as you want to throw at it.

THE CARS

Today's modern sprint car is the result of more than a half-century of evolution. Its characteristics differ little from one region of the country to another. It has an 89-inch wheelbase and weighs in the neighborhood of 1,200 pounds. Weight has been a controversial issue, because several groups have attempted to control the cost of racing by establishing a minimum weight rule. Others in the sport contend that using current materials and technology, a car weighs less than 1,200 pounds right off the manufacturer's floor.

A sprint car's frame sides are joined with braces in the stand–up jig. *Randy Jones*

The most popular sprint car engine is a fuel-injected short-block Chevy 410. Ford and Mopar build similar powerplants for racing. The top engines all exceed 800 horsepower. Methanol is used for fuel. Power is transmitted through a torque tube to a direct-drive rear end. The cars have an in/out gearbox, meaning it is either in gear or not. It is designed to allow the crews to make quick gear changes at the track.

In outward appearance, most sprint cars are the same; they have undergone few dramatic changes in appearance. One innovation used in recent years involved making the nose of the car more aerodynamic by creating a snubby, rounded contour. In some applications, this required relocating the radiator to a vertical position sitting sideways in the frame.

Another new approach, debuted by J & J in 2001, incorporated several changes that aid aerodynamics, including laying the radiator horizontally under the nose to keep clean air flowing. Jack Elam, founder of J & J, explained that until recently, moving the air properly around a sprint car wasn't important because they have few flat surfaces on the bottom of the car. Now, in addition to making the cars more streamlined, designers are employing aerodynamics to help the engines run cooler and make them more efficient.

Chevy's short-block 410 has been the popular choice of sprint car racers for years. *Randy Jones*

BUILDING A SPRINT CAR

The number of manufacturers of sprint cars changes every year. Some are regional and produce very small numbers, while others have been in business for many years and support the national market. The best-known sprint car builders include Maxim, J & J, Eagle, Gambler, Stealth, Avenger, and Schnee.

Indianapolis-based Stealth Motorsports was founded by New Zealander John Godfrey in 1992. General Manager Marc Dailey says Stealth builds about 300 sprint cars a year, which are divided between the winged and the non-winged markets. He estimates that between 250 and 400 winged Stealth sprint cars are being raced every summer.

Stealth's manufacturing facility in northern Indianapolis is housed in several connected buildings. One contains the speed shop, handling retail sales of everything from completed sprint cars and parts to accessories and clothing. In the large frame shop, a dozen frames of various types stand on end, waiting to be inspected and refurbished. Chassis nearing completion are lined up at one end. Jigs around the room hold various types of frames in different stages of construction. Stealth builds a variety of chassis for open-wheel racers, from silver crown machines to quarter-midgets and micro-sprint cars.

Building a sprint car chassis takes about 24 man-hours. The chassis begins life as 24- to 28-foot lengths of chrome-moly (molybdenum), a lightweight steel alloy tubing. The tubes are cut and precisely curved to specific contours using a Hostfield bender, a machine designed specifically for shaping steel tubing.

After cutting and shaping, the tubing is set into a side jig. This jig, designed for welding the frame sides together, consists of a specially built table with a smoothly polished half-inch steel plate tabletop. The table has levelers and rollers to keep it level while it is moved around the shop floor. Bins built into place under the tabletop are kept stocked with the smaller braces and pieces of tubing that are added to the frame to provide strength and support. This way they are within easy reach of the welder working on the frame.

Movable aluminum blocks, called saddles, are shaped to hold the tubing and lock it into position with bolts. When a dozen or so saddles are positioned and bolted in the right spots on the

This is how every sprint car starts out, chrome-moly tubing waiting to be cut and bent. *Randy Jones*

After being shaped, the frame sides are constructed in a flat jig. *Randy Jones*

53

It takes about 24 cumulative hours of labor to build a sprint car chassis. *Randy Jones*

side jig, the shaped lengths of tubing will lay in them. The pieces of the frame side are fitted and then welded together.

When the left and the right sides of the frame are complete, they are moved to the stand-up jig. There the frame tubing that runs across the chassis, connecting the left and right sides, is tacked in place. Other pieces, like the engine plate, are also added. When the frame tacking is completed it is moved to a finishing jig, where final welding is performed. This includes adding tank mounts, wing tabs, and bars for additional arm protection if desired.

The car builders work on several cars at once. While one fabricator is performing the final welding,

Rough edges of the frame are smoothed out on the finishing table. *Randy Jones*

Color, with a finish that can't be chipped, can now be introduced to fiberglass pieces during fabrication, alleviating the need for painting. *Randy Jones*

another will work on the side frames for the next car to be built. Another worker might be busy measuring and cutting the smaller pieces that fill the bins under the jigs.

Daily says that Stealth is the only sprint car manufacturer that makes its own fiberglass body parts. Building the body pieces begins by creating a buck, which is a piece of foam, aluminum, or plywood that is shaped and sanded into the desired shape. Then a fiberglass mold is cast from the buck.

Building the body pieces begins by spraying a polyester gelcoat into the mold. A colored epoxy resin is added, followed by matte and cloth. When the mixture hardens, the piece is snapped out of the mold and rough edges are trimmed. Holes are added so the piece can be attached to the car.

Generally, the completed product begins with the frame and fiberglass body panels. Each manufacturer sells kits ranging from basic to deluxe packages. The kits add many of the items that will need to be installed on the car to make it race-ready, but are available from a variety of aftermarket sources in addition to the manufacturer. Items that are available in kits generally include the aluminum dash, floor pan, axles, pedals, steering mount, torsion arms, tie rods, steering arms, radiator box, sway bar, radius rods, drag link, birdcages, clevis assembly, Jacobs ladder, bumpers, and nerf bars.

THE RACE TEAM

The assembly is performed at the racer's facility. This includes installing the engine, brakes, shocks, steering gear, fuel tank and bladder, gauges, shifter assembly, power steering, oil tank, radiator, seat and safety equipment, and wings. The racer can buy many of these components from Stealth or the other manufacturers, or from companies that specialize in

Finished parts are waiting to be shipped. These will be included with kits and installed at the race team's shop. *Randy Jones*

INNOVATION, PROGRESS, AND SAFETY

Karl Kinser is frequently given credit for being one of the most important innovators in sprint car racing. With the record he compiled before and since the founding of the World of Outlaws, there is no doubt about his contribution to the sprint car's evolution. Karl's had a unique ability to conceive better ways of doing many different types of things. At the same time, he could evaluate an idea that someone else was trying and then adapt it to his car. Clearly, individual innovations and changes he made were important, but the cumulative effect of adding small changes made his chassis very effective.

He found that experimenting with different ways of doing things often resulted in faster cars and races won. He also realized that better and safer race cars made more money. As an example, he is credited with making the downtube sprint car design (on which frame rails extend from the top of the roll cage to the front of the frame) a winner. He explains, "Every time you'd crash a nondowntube car, it would just bend the frame up and you'd junk the frame from the motor plate forward. The downtube was just something that would make the car a lot more of a trussed effect. In other words, it's harder to bend. That's where it came up. And once I built one, it was, in my mind, far safer for the driver. It just gives the driver more protection, and if the car's stouter, it's just harder to tear it apart."

With all of his innovations, Kinser claims that the major advancements came in the use of lighter and stronger materials. "Back in the late 1950s and early 1960s, we used all steel arms, steel axles. They came out with better aluminum alloy, and it just made the cars faster and actually safer. You take a sprint car that weighed 2,200 pounds and if you turned that thing over, end over end, it don't stop as quick as say a 1,200-pound car. And that makes the car safer for the driver, plus you don't tear up as many parts.

"So the theory of a heavy race car is not quite what people think it is. I'd rather race an 800-pound car, if I could. The simple reason is that you don't change the structure of what the driver is sitting in. You change the parts around him. And if the parts absorb more energy by bending, like the front axle, flats, and radius rods, and things like that, and the wing, it takes the energy of the crash away from the driver. So a big heavy race car, it takes more to bend it, but the driver is sitting inside of it and he gets the shock. That's why you have far fewer injuries in racing now. Take, for instance, Eldora. Eldora's over 3.5 seconds faster than it was 20 years ago, and you don't have near as many people hurt at Eldora as you used to. All of that has got to be telling you something."

these parts. Frequently, the top teams will have special designs fabricated or sponsorship arrangements with these companies.

Karl Kinser's approach is to order bare frames from Maxim. Everything else either comes from other sources, or he builds it himself. The assembly process is straightforward, Karl says. "We paint the frames and weld all of the body fasteners on it and put the type of

Completed chassis stand on end at Stealth Motorsports, waiting for delivery. *Randy Jones*

brake pedal in it that suits the driver the best. Beyond that it's just bolting the rest of the components on the frame and lining the car up. By the time you get a new one and get it painted, just say you stayed on one car and had all the parts, you're looking at a week."

While some teams buy nearly complete sprint car kits, others begin with a bare frame and assemble their preferred components. *Randy Jones*

The crews that maintain the sprint cars aren't large. They range in size from the driver who does all the work by himself, to a team consisting of a crew chief and several crewmen.

Next to the driver, the crew chief is most responsible for the team's success. The best crew chiefs perform on a variety of levels and allow the driver to focus on his job. He helps build the cars during the off season. He has spent years on the road learning how to take care of a car properly. He must also master the art of reading the tracks as proficiently as the drivers and know how to effectively adjust the car's setup for changing conditions. He also learns effective techniques for making quick repairs in the pits.

In describing a top crew chief, Donny Schatz outlined the responsibility that Kenny Woodruff has with his team. "A good crew chief is able to not only run the race team and get the race cars set up, he is able to deal with the politics and make decisions. They also should be involved with the paperwork, with the billing processes, and paying for things. Pretty much running everything from the ground up. Kenny drives the truck, he does the race car, and he organizes the crew."

Karl Kinser may be the foremost crew chief of all time, and his definition of the job is memorable. "He brings the knowledge of all the years that he's been into it. You take a good one and the guy ain't 20 years

Axles and rear ends are among the many components that can be purchased from manufacturers that specialize in sprint car equipment. *Randy Jones*

old, he's probably 50. So it's just more knowledge than the younger sprint car team manager or crew chief. It's kind of ironic, all the older guys around the race track, the young ones call them old dudes or old geezers. And then if they want to know something about the race car they don't go ask their 20-year-old buddy, they come around and they say, 'O One of Great Knowledge.' The guys who have been there the longest have more common knowledge of the racing.

He doesn't make the same mistake twice. The older pit crews and crew chiefs win most of the races. They win the most in Indy car races, the most in sprint and in NASCAR. It's no different, it's just that actually racing is a lot of, let's call it an educated guess. You won't be right every time, but you'll be more right more. It's relatively simple. You get out here and you become a good crew chief in 10 years, you don't do it in the first one."

Initial investment:
Truck and trailer
(new—hey, you won the lottery) $150,000
Two race- ready sprint cars
@ about $30,000 $60,000
Two competitive racing engines
@ at least $40,000 $80,000

This is just a start. You also may have to outfit a shop with equipment and tools. You'll need a tool set and a four-wheeler or mule to take to the track. And you will probably need another engine before the season is over.

By now, you should have started putting together a crew. Kenny Jacobs recommends, "You're going to have to have one good mechanic, or you automatically don't have a chance to win. And then you've got to have a really good go-getter of a youngster, a kid who'll dive in with both feet, get up in the morning and not complain and do whatever you ask him to do. You've got to have at least two people. And then you've got to go out and find yourself a good driver, or you'll run out of money before you can imagine. If you don't have those three ingredients, you'll go through all your racing equipment so fast your head will be spinning."

| Crew chief | $2,000–$3,500 per month |
| Crewman | $1,000–$1,500 per month |

When you are on the road, you have to include their motel rooms and other expenses. Plus you have to pay withholding and other employer-related taxes.

A good driver will probably race for a percentage of the winnings and part of any appearance money. A common figure is 40 percent of what the car earns, and 50 percent if he wins. Some may require a retainer, or salary, in addition to the percentage.

There are other expenses every time you unload your car. Pit passes will range from $20 to $50 per person. Tires, fuel, and oil will be consumed. If you tear something up it will have to be replaced.

Axles, radiator, brakes, shocks, steering gear, fuel tank and bladder, seat, and safety equipment are installed at the race team's shop. *Randy Jones*

A PLAN FOR RACING

Okay, you won the lottery, let's go racing. Here is a budget that will allow us to race two or three times a weekend, and put a competitive car on the track. And, maybe win a little money back.

Karl Kinser's crew can make a race-ready car from a bare frame in about a week. *Randy Jones*

As many people who decide to go racing learn, there are too many variables to accurately budget a year of racing. However, this outline tells you that you could probably spend $300,000 to $500,000 if you do it right. The cost decreases after the first year, because the initial investment in the truck and trailer and the tools has already been made.

The majority of sprint car racers are able to compete with less expenditure. They know where to buy used equipment, and where they can save money without sacrificing too much performance. There are less expensive engines. But the bottom line remains, "Speed costs money. How fast do you want to go?"

LIFE ON THE ROAD

Racing is the life that sprint car drivers and mechanics have chosen, and during the racing season nearly everything they do focuses on their cars and the next race.

BEFORE THE NEXT RACE

Most teams have developed a standard routine that they follow between races. It begins immediately after they finish the feature race as they load the equipment and the car. Once out of the track, their first stop is usually a car wash.

"We do that after the race every night," Kenny Jacobs explained. "We find a car wash somewhere, and we unload half the trailer and the car and make sure everything's as spotless as we can get it. And we try to dry everything to keep it from water-spotting. That way when you get working the next morning, the car's dried completely and the seat

Karl Kinser enjoys working on his cars in the motel parking lot. It gives the public a closer look at what more than 800 horsepower looks like. *Randy Jones*

A motel parking lot can become a busy place when the racers are in town for a big event. *Randy Jones*

and the belts are starting to dry, and you're not working on a wet race car."

Even though it's well after midnight by the time the crew members get to their motel, they are up early the next morning. An early start will allow them to finish their work before the hottest part of the afternoon. Usually, a team has a maintenance routine that is critical to keeping its equipment operating properly. Frequently the motel parking lot or a highway rest area allows room to unload the equipment and begin work.

Jacobs, whose standard maintenance is probably typical, describes what his team does before the next race. "We start by dismounting all the tires that we ran the night before. We'll keep one set of good used tires to hot lap on. The others are dismounted, folded, numbered, and put in the front of the trailer. We mount new tires, and we groove them the way we want them grooved. We change the gear. We pull the driveline loose and clean and

Crews will either grow close or split apart while traveling and working together. Donny Schatz and Kenny Woodruff have formed a successful team. *Randy Jones*

Tires are expensive, but critical to the car's performance. Every crew makes sure that its tires are ready to go. *Randy Jones*

lubricate the bell housing. We grease the car. We change the oil every three races and we change the filter every two races. We maintenance the motor, and we run the valves. We leak-test the motor down and make sure we're not having a problem with a head gasket or a radiator leak or anything like that. We usually have another set of filters clean and ready to put on the car. When the filters are all changed, we just look at everything on the car. We maintenance the birdcages about every other night and make sure they look good. The inside of the trailer and the truck get cleaned out every day. That's part of the maintenance routine."

Maintenance, a word that racers like Kenny Jacobs regularly employ as a verb, encompasses many actions. In a single word, it describes processes of inspecting, turning, twisting, measuring, thumping, adjusting, and lubricating everything from the wheel assemblies to engine components.

Another important task is checking the safety equipment. The safety harnesses are inspected to make sure that they aren't starting to fray or bind, and the bolts holding the seat in place are checked to be sure they're still tight. Other equipment is also inspected and replaced if necessary.

GETTING DOWN THE ROAD

Often the teams will have to travel several hundred miles between races, and as soon as the maintenance is completed, they are on the road. If they don't have time to stop, they can eat and change into clean clothes when they get to the track. This demanding lifestyle will either draw the team's mechanics and driver closer together, or it will amplify friction among them. Usually when team members aren't getting along, changes will happen quickly.

There was a time when sprint cars were towed around the country on open trailers, hooked to a station wagon or pickup truck. With basically just a driver and mechanic, all of the team's tools and equipment, spare parts, and clothes were on the trailer or in the back of their vehicle. As they put miles behind them, traveling from town to town, it wasn't unusual for the car or truck to serve as a motel room and makeshift office.

While the number of miles a racing team covers in a year has changed little, travel for today's drivers, mechanics, and equipment has certainly been upgraded. The enclosed trailers are spacious, and their size and appointments are limited only by the budget. They come with traditional trailer hitches,

fifth wheel, or gooseneck designs, ranging in overall length from 32 feet (two axles) to 53 feet (three axles).

Race trailers are designed to transport the sprint car, spares, equipment, and tools, and the larger ones even have a lounge area. For many teams, the tractor that tows the trailer is large enough to also have accommodations for sleeping.

A sprint car, with the wing removed, can be rolled right into the trailer. The four-wheeled mule

A cross-section of a well-equipped sprint car trailer

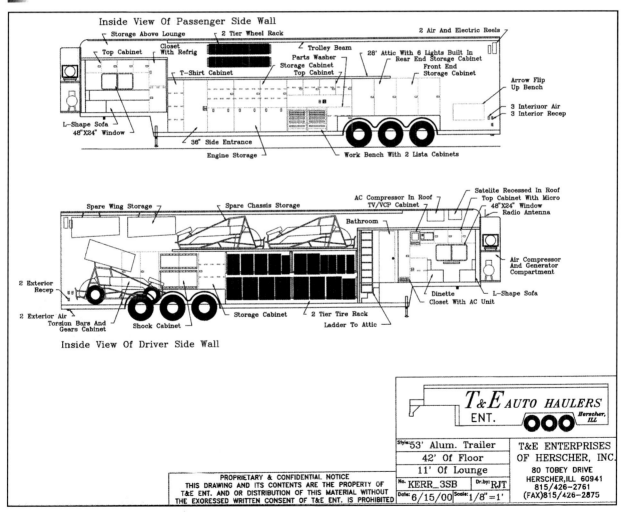

that is used to push the car around the infield and carry parts and tools for quick repairs, also fits right on the floor of the trailer. With shelves and cabinets along the walls, it is a tight fit, but once the car is rolled out of the trailer, the crew has room to work.

When the top sprint car teams go on the road for extended trips, they'll usually carry one or two complete "rollers," cars ready to go on the track with everything except an engine. There will usually be another spare chassis and enough parts to prepare up to six more chassis.

It isn't unusual to also carry as many as six engines, stored under a counter and ready to drop into a sprint car, with all the clamps, hoses, and bolt-on accessories already in place.

If the team wrecked its car the night before, it will either repair it or build a new one from parts it carries before going to the next race. Local racers may allow them to use their garages and help with welding and straightening. Often preparing a new car is quicker, and it is usually a matter of installing an engine in one of the rollers, then adding some incidental parts such as the driver's seat and safety equipment. In extreme cases, the team can start with a nearly bare frame that it carries and build up a car

Once everything is organized, there is plenty of room to work inside today's sprint car trailers. *Randy Jones*

The top teams carry several chassis when they go on the road. Note the "roller" that can quickly be pressed into service, conveniently stored on an overhead shelf. *Randy Jones*

SAFETY EQUIPMENT

Racers stake their lives on their safety equipment. Whenever they work on the car, whether at the track or in a motel parking lot, they quickly look at their safety belts. Everything else is evaluated regularly. Kenny Jacobs discusses his concern for safety and safety equipment.

"I've never had even a slightest problem with any of my safety equipment. Absolutely none. The Simpson belts that I've run for years I've had zero trouble with. I've been running Crow safety belts for the last two years. They're just bulletproof. The Butlerbuilt seats are the same way—you can't hurt one of them. I never worry about a helmet. I usually go through three helmets a season, because they get beat up so bad by rocks that you'll find hairline cracks in the face part. I replace them when that happens. Or if I were to take a blow to the head, I'll replace the helmet. I wouldn't wear it anymore. Other than that, my wife takes care of all of the fireproof driver's uniforms. She takes care of the laundry and I try to hand dry them as much as I can."

in a few hours. With few exceptions, everything it needs is carried in the trailer.

FAMILY LIFE

On some teams the driver is an essential part of the crew. He works on the car every day and may even help drive the hauler. On other teams, the crew chief and mechanics take care of everything. Depending on his own preferences and situation, the driver may travel with the team or take his own motor home. Donny Schatz explains, "At times I travel with the team and leave my motor home at home. It's nonsense to take the motor home on long drives. But it's awful nice to have a motor home that allows me to get a break, get away, but still be in touch with the race team."

Schatz's crew chief, Kenny Woodruff, travels with his wife, Annie, who helps the team with many duties, including selling Donny's merchandise at the track. During a long summer on the road, it isn't unusual for the driver to take his wife and family with him. The modern motor coach has nearly all of the amenities that the family is used to at home.

Life on the road can be arduous. Dale Blaney waits until he needs to climb back into his machine.
Randy Jones

Many drivers travel with their families in motor homes. On race weekend, a small village sprouts near the pit area.
Randy Jones

Craig and Julie Dollansky and their children are veterans of the sprint car highway. Although the family has spent the whole season with the racing team in the past, the children are now old enough to be in school. Julie says now there are times that they all travel and others when the family stays home while Craig races.

What do they miss most while on the road? The kids may have a different answer, but Julie quickly says "washing machines and dryers." Then she adds "and post offices."

When they take their three youngsters on the road, the kids sleep on pull-out couches in the front of the motor home, and there is a slide-out master bedroom in

A home away from home for many racers, the comfort of the motor home is reflected in mirrors. *Randy Jones*

the back. Cooking while on the highway is just one example of the many things about the life that can be a challenge until mastered. The experienced traveler will have a neighbor or family member back home who ships things ahead to hotels along their route.

Julie Dollansky says it's definitely not a normal life. "It's not all the fun and games that people think it is. It's still a business." She points out that they might get to their Elk River, Minnesota, home three times, for a day each, the whole summer. Most sprint car teams are small businesses, and if the driver is also the team manager, there isn't a lot of leisure time on the road. They still have to keep records and pay bills, so their motor home also serves as an office.

After long periods on the road, most crewmen and their families look forward to getting back home. But being racers, they will soon begin thinking about the next race.

After long periods on the road, race teams are anxious to return home. This is Karl Kinser's shop in Indiana. *Randy Jones*

BIG EVENTS AND THE FAMILY JEWELS

Almost by definition, sprint car racers are money racers. From the very first time they climb through the roll cage, they are all about winning—outrunning the other guys to the checkered flag. Without exception, they would trade 2,000 points for the opportunity to stand on the victory stage at the Knoxville Nationals, the biggest sprint car race of all. Certain events have grown in stature because of the big payoff, the closeness of the competition among the sport's best cars and drivers, and the electricity in the air as fans pack the grandstands early.

Danny Smith (12x) and Jac Haudenschild battle at Eldora. *Randy Jones*

Lady Liberty is part of the pageantry of the Knoxville Nationals. *Randy Jones*

THE MONEY RACES

The Knoxville Nationals have become the most important week in sprint car racing. Teams begin planning and preparing months in advance, carefully selecting engines and chassis, and evaluating every component in their racing programs. With nearly 150 racing cars on hand at Knoxville Raceway, the Nationals consists of three consecutive nights of racing and qualifying, all to gain points for starting positions in Saturday's final program. After 30 circuits of the half-mile oval, the winner's paycheck is $125,000, the biggest in sprint car racing.

Steve Kinser finds it difficult to suppress his emotions after winning the 1994 Knoxville Nationals. *Randy Jones*

Racing is always close at Knoxville. Here Danny Young battles Jerry Reichert Jr. during the 1994 Nationals. *Randy Jones*

WINNERS OF THE KNOXVILLE NATIONALS

2001 Danny Lasoski
2000 Mark Kinser
1999 Mark Kinser
1998 Danny Lasoski
1997 Dave Blaney
1996 Mark Kinser
1995 Steve Kinser
1994 Steve Kinser
1993 Steve Kinser
1992 Steve Kinser
1991 Steve Kinser
1990 Bobby Allen
1989 Doug Wolfgang

1988 Steve Kinser
1987 Steve Kinser
1986 Steve Kinser
1985 Doug Wolfgang
1984 Doug Wolfgang
1983 Sammy Swindell
1982 Steve Kinser
1981 Steve Kinser
1980 Steve Kinser
1979 Ron Shuman
1978 Doug Wolfgang
1977 Doug Wolfgang
1976 Eddie Leavitt
1975 Eddie Leavitt
1974 Dick Gaines

Busy pits at Eldora. *Randy Jones*

1973 Kenny Weld
1972 Kenny Weld
1971 Jan Opperman
1970 Joe Saldana
1969 Kenny Gritz
1968 Ray Lee Goodwin
1967 Thad Dosher
1966 Jay Woodside
1965 Kenny Weld
1964 Kenny Weld
1963 Greg Weld
1962 Jerry Richert, Sr.
1961 Roy Robbins

Eldora Speedway's owner, Earl Baltes, knows that to make headlines, you have to lure the top racers and reward them with a big check. In 1993, he initiated the first $100,000-to-win sprint car race in the country and dubbed it The Historical Big One.

Steve Kinser races Jac Haudenschild during the Historical Big One at Eldora. *Randy Jones*

On consecutive nights before the HBO, Eldora hosts the All Stars and the World of Outlaws. But the big event is open to anyone who tows into the track.

WINNERS OF THE HISTORICAL BIG ONE
2001 P. J. Chesson
2000 Steve Kinser
1999 Kevin Gobrecht
1998 Dale Blaney
1997 Dave Blaney
1996 Mark Kinser
1995 Steve Kinser
1994 Kenny Jacobs
1993 Jac Haudenschild

For one night in June, the King's Royal brings pageantry and nobility to rural Ohio. Traditionally, the winner is treated like royalty, as the $50,000 paycheck is presented only after he has been regally robed and crowned on a stage illuminated by flaming torches and filled with tradition.

WINNERS OF THE KING'S ROYAL
2001 Mark Kinser
2000 Dale Blaney
1999 Sammy Swindell
1998 Jac Haudenschild
1997 Steve Kinser
1996 Johnny Herrera
1995 Dave Blaney
1994 Jac Haudenschild
1993 Dave Blaney
1992 Sammy Swindell
1991 Steve Kinser
1990 Doug Wolfgang
1989 Bobby Davis Jr.
1988 Steve Kinser
1987 Jac Haudenschild
1986 Don Kreitz
1985 Doug Wolfgang
1984 Steve Kinser

This is only part of the booty. The King's Royal trophy carries a $50,000 payday with it. *Randy Jones*

The Terre Haute Action Track half-mile, located at the Vigo County Fairgrounds, was built in 1949. Joey Saldana, Jac Haudenschild (22), and Danny Wood show that there are three ways to get through Turn Three. *Randy Jones*

The Don Martin Memorial Silver Cup is more than just one stop in sprint car racing's "month of money." Conceived by track promoter Don Martin, the first Silver Cup event was run on Lernerville Speedway's 25th Anniversary and paid $25,000 to Sammy Swindell. Martin added another $1,000 to the winner's check each year, and after his death the Martin family has continued the tradition. Mark Kinser, with his victory in 2001, earned $34,000.

WINNERS OF THE DON MARTIN MEMORIAL SILVER CUP

2001 Mark Kinser
2000 Sammy Swindell
1999 Mark Kinser
1998 Mark Kinser
1997 Mark Kinser
1996 Mark Kinser
1995 Stevie Smith
1994 Steve Kinser
1993 Jeff Swindell
1992 Sammy Swindell

One of the biggest events in Pennsylvania's busy racing season has always been the Williams Grove National Open. Like the Knoxville Nationals, The Open has been filling the grandstands ever since the days of super-modifieds. It's winners list reads like an honor roll of open-wheel racing history.

WINNERS OF THE WILLIAMS GROVE NATIONAL OPEN

2001 Lance Dewease
2000 Donny Schatz
1999 Mark Kinser
1998 Billy Pauch
1997 Sammy Swindell
1996 Lance Dewease
1995 Mark Kinser
1994 Steve Kinser
1993 Don Kreitz Jr.
1992 Steve Kinser
1991 Stevie Smith Jr.
1990 Steve Kinser
1989 Stevie Smith Jr.
1988 Kenny Jacobs
1987 Joey Allen
1986 Doug Wolfgang
1985 Doug Wolfgang
1984 Doug Wolfgang
1983 Lynn Paxton
1982 Lynn Paxton

1981 Steve Smith
1980 Allen Klinger
1979 Smokey Snellbaker
1978 Kramer Williamson
1977 Van May
1976 Steve Smith
1975 Bobby Allen
1974 Steve Smith
1973 Kenny Weld
1972 Kenny Weld
1971 Kenny Weld
1970 Johnny Crum
1969 Gene Varner
1968 Bobby Adamson
1967 Bobby Adamson
1966 Lou Blaney
1965 Henry Jacoby
1964 Larry Dickson
1963 Gordon Johncock

California's Gold Cup Race of Champions has been competed annually since 1951. Originally a stock car event, it was frequently a 100- or 200-lap marathon. The Gold Cup switched to sprint cars at West Capital Raceway in 1973, and since 1980 has been held on the quarter-mile at Silver Dollar Speedway in Chico.

GOLD CUP CHAMPIONS

2001 Mark Kinser
2000 Danny Lasoski
1999 Jac Haudenschild
1998 Jac Haudenschild
1997 Dave Blaney
1996 Jeff Swindell
1995 Andy Hillenburg
1994 Andy Hillenburg
1993 Stevie Smith
1992 Steve Kinser
1991 Joe Gaerte
1990 Steve Kinser
1989 Darrell Hanestad

Bloomington Speedway's rich red clay is a trademark of the quarter-mile oval in southern Indiana. Danny Smith turns a quick lap while qualifying. *Randy Jones*

1988 Steve Kinser
1987 Steve Kinser
1986 Steve Kinser
1985 Danny Smith
1984 Steve Kinser
1983 Steve Kinser
1982 Doug Wolfgang
1981 Sammy Swindell
1980 Johnny Anderson
1979 Steve Kinser
1978 Steve Kinser
1977 Gary Patterson
1976 LeRoy VanConett
1975 Terry Crousure
1974 Johnny Anderson
1973 Jimmy Boyd

The home of the Hoosier Fall Classic, Lawrenceburg Speedway, is located on the Ohio River in the southeastern corner of Indiana. As the leaves begin to change color in the southern Indiana hills, the $10,000-to-win event marks the final races of the All Stars calendar.

WINNERS OF THE HOOSIER FALL CLASSIC

2001 Dean Jacobs
2000 Danny Smith
1999 Chad Kemenah
1998 Kenny Jacobs
1997 Gary Wright
1996 Kelly Kinser
1995 (rained out)
1994 Danny Lasoski
1993 Mark Kinser
1992 Kevin Huntley
1991 Rick Hood
1990 Kelly Kinser
1989 Robbie Stanley
1988 Joe Gaerte
1987 Kelly Kinser & Kevin Huntley
1986 Dave Blaney

1985 Tim Green
1984 Jack Hewitt
1983 Lee Osborne

For two weeks every February, sprint car teams head to Florida for the All Stars Sprint Speedweeks action. The winter racing attracts top drivers from around the country to Volusia Speedway Park, outside of Daytona Beach, and East Bay Raceway, near Tampa. New teams make their first forays together, while others try out the latest equipment. Speedweeks concludes with the hotly contested East Bay Winternationals, where the $26,000 winner's share will cover the cost of the Florida vacation.

WINNERS OF THE EAST BAY WINTERNATIONALS

2001 Gary Wright
2000 Danny Lasoski
1999 Jeff Shepard
1998 Jeff Shepard
1997 Brian Schnee
1996 Bill Brian Jr.
1995 Lance Dewease
1994 Stevie Smith
1993 Keith Kauffman
1992 Bobby Davis Jr.
1991 Kenny Jacobs
1990 Randy Wolfe
1989 Steve Smith
1988 Paul Lotier
1987 Bobby Davis Jr.
1986 Bobby Davis Jr.
1985 Bobby Davis Jr.
1984 Sammy Swindell
1983 Steve Kinser
1982 Sammy Swindell
1981 Doug Wolfgang
1980 Doug Wolfgang
1979 Doug Wolfgang
1978 Doug Wolfgang
1977 Paul Pitzer

SPRINT SPEEDWEEK

Two of the most anticipated sprint car events of each summer, Pennsylvania Speedweek and Ohio Sprint Speedweek, bring out the best in drivers and crews. A series of consecutive races, each night at a different track, provides tremendous challenges for racing teams. Frequently accompanied by the midsummer rainstorms that yield temporary relief from the heat, teams work feverishly to keep cars ready for the next race. If a car is torn up, it is an all-night thrash to prepare a new one. In addition to a payday every night, racers vie for a bonus that goes to the Speedweek champion.

All Stars Ohio Sprint Speedweek Champions

2001 Dean Jacobs	1991 Sammy Swindell
2000 Kenny Jacobs	1990 Sammy Swindell
1999 Joey Saldana	1989 Dave Blaney
1998 Frankie Kerr	1988 Jimmy Sills
1997 Joey Saldana	1987 Keith Kauffman
1996 Frankie Kerr	1986 Bobby Allen
1995 Dale Blaney	1985 Jack Hewitt
1994 Frankie Kerr	1984 Steve Kinser
1993 Frankie Kerr	1983 Bobby Davis Jr.
1992 Kevin Huntley	

The top sprint car drivers in California compete for the King of California crown in a series of races at various tracks. Brent Kaeding has dominated these events, winning 11 of 16 championships.

KING OF CALIFORNIA

2001 Brent Kaeding	1993 Brent Kaeding
2000 Ronnie Day	1992 Tim Green
1999 Brent Kaeding	1991 Brent Kaeding
1998 Randy Hannagan	1990 Brent Kaeding
1997 Brent Kaeding	1989 Brent Kaeding
1996 Brent Kaeding	1988 Brent Kaeding
1995 Brent Kaeding	1987 Steve Kent
1994 Brent Kaeding	1986 Steve Kent

THE RACE TRACKS

One element that differentiates sprint car racing from other sports is that the venues are the family jewels of the sport. Each one is distinct in character, atmosphere, landscape, and racing attributes. They

Leland McSpadden is on the gas during the Western World Championship at Phoenix's Manzanita Speedway in 1991. *Randy Jones*

reflect the natural characteristics of their surroundings, whether high in the mountains, at an oasis in the desert, or part of a motorsports megaplex. Many of them have been kept in the same family for generations, providing tradition that racers respect.

Each race track is unique. Some are very unusual, while others have subtle differences. The most experienced drivers and chief mechanics have an advantage because they are better able to take advantage of the nuances of each oval. They predict more accurately how natural forces, such as like the sun, shadows, wind, or moisture, will affect certain parts of each track and how the racing surface is apt to change during a complete racing program.

Savvy racing fans are likewise knowledgeable of the characteristics of each facility. While some are located in beautiful rural settings, others are found in industrial parks. Fans discover favorite places to sit, the best areas to camp, where to park, and where to eat.

One of the most visible tracks in sprint car racing is Iowa's Knoxville Raceway, home of the annual Knoxville Nationals. Promoter Ralph Capitani and the town of Knoxville welcome thousands of visitors to its weekly sprint car programs each summer. With wide, slightly banked turns, Knoxville's half-mile gives drivers room to race. As a result, many top drivers, including Danny Lasoski, Craig Dollansky, Johnny Herrera, Terry McCarl, and Skip Jackson came through the ranks at Knoxville. The historic National Sprint Car Hall of Fame and Museum is located outside of turn two.

Earl Baltes constructed Eldora Speedway in a western Ohio cornfield in the late 1950s. Since then the high-banked half-mile has been a home for high-speed sprint car competition. A brilliant promoter, Baltes was one of the first to make high-paying sprint car races profitable. His King's Royal and Historical Big One weekends attract standing-room-only crowds that fill the parking lots with campers.

The sprint car tracks in Pennsylvania take on the characteristics of the native mountain surroundings. They are as rural and rustic as they are big and fast. For years, the Pennsylvania circuit has seen little change. Williams Grove Speedway (Mechanicsburg) and Lernerville (Sarver) host on Friday nights. Saturday sprint goers have a choice between Lincoln (Hanover), Port Royal, and Selinsgrove. Susquehanna was a Sunday night staple for years, although it isn't currently active. Although it's physically located across the border in Maryland, Hagerstown is considered part of the Pennsylvania circuit when it hosts sprint cars.

Lincoln Speedway is in its fifth decade as a pillar of the Pennsylvania Posse. *Jack Kromer*

Located in Maryland, spectacular Hagerstown Speedway is included in the Pennsylvania circuit when sprint cars are on the card. *Jack Kromer*

Before switching to NASCAR's Winston Cup circuit, Dave Blaney won the Outlaws championship. Here, he is at the site of the Outlaws' first race, Devil's Bowl Speedway, in 1996. *Randy Jones*

Ohio and Indiana present an active sprint car scene. In addition to Eldora, Ohio's facilities are the summer home of the All Stars and include Attica Raceway, Sharon Speedway (Hartford), Fremont Speedway, K-C Raceway (Chillicothe), Wayne County Speedway (Orrville), Limaland Motorsports Park (Lima), and Portsmouth Raceway. Across the border, the Terre Haute Action Track, Bloomington Speedway, Tri-State Speedway in Haubstadt, and Lawrenceburg Speedway also host periodic winged sprint car events.

California's Golden State Challenge visits Chico's Silver Dollar Speedway, King's Speedway in Hanford, the Tulare Thunderbowl, and Speedways in Placerville, Santa Maria, Calistoga, and Bakersfield.

"Manzy" (Manzanita Speedway) is located in the southwest suburbs of Phoenix, near the Salt River. A historic half-mile oval with long straightaways and lightning-fast turns, Manzanita has been home to the Western World Championship race since the 1960s. Located in an industrial area with a predominantly Mexican flavor, the track takes advantage of the distinct southwestern characteristics in its architecture and atmosphere. Once the sun goes down, it's the coolest place in Phoenix.

Other tracks in the West continue to thrive. Among them are Mesquite's Devil's Bowl Speedway, State Fair Park in Oklahoma City, Eagle Raceway in Nebraska, Skagit Speedway in Washington, and Red River Valley in West Fargo, North Dakota.

In recent years, modern facilities have been built at Las Vegas Motor Speedway, Lake Perris (California), Fort Worth's Texas Motor Speedway, the Talladega Short Track (Alabama), Heartland Park in Topeka (Kansas), and Lowes Motor Speedway in Concord (North Carolina) to host sprint car racing. Although they may be a direction of the future, they will never supplant the traditional ovals.

APPENDIX

THE SPRINT CAR HALL OF FAME

(* deceased)

1990

Larry Dickson
Tommy Hinnershitz*
Floyd Trevis*
Jan Opperman*
J.C. Agajanian*
A.J. Foyt Jr.
Jack Gunn*
Gus Schrader*
Wilbur Shaw*
Arthur Chevrolet*
Louis Chevrolet*
Floyd "Pop" Dreyer*
August Duesenberg*
Fred Duesenberg*
Ralph Hankinson*
Frank Lockhart*
Rex Mays*
Harry A. Miller*
Barney Oldfield*
J. Alex Sloan*

1991

Ralph DePalma*
Louis Meyer*
Dennis "Duke" Nalon*
Ernie Triplett*
Emory Collins*
Ted Horn*
Parnelli Jones
Hector Honore*

Jerry Richert, Sr.*
Art Sparks*
"Bud" Winfield*
Ed Winfield*
Don Edmunds
Frank Funk*
Fred J. "Pop" Wagner*
Al Sweeney*
Marion Robinson*
Duane "Pancho" Carter Jr.

1992

Art Pillsbury*
Rich Vogler*
Bobby Grim*
John C. Vance*
Alex Morales*
Tony Willman*
Earl B. Gilmore*
Ennis "Dizz" Wilson*
Dick Gaines*
Sheldon Kinser*
T.E. "Pop" Myers*
Sam Nunis*
Jud Larson*
Tommy Milton*
Eddie Rickenbacker*
John B. Gerber*
Ronnie Allyn*
Bob Sall*

1993

Lloyd Axel*
Gary Bettenhausen

Steve (11) and Mark Kinser race during the Sprint Car World Series at Canyon Speedway. *Randy Jones*

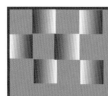

SUMMARY OF THE WORLD
OF OUTLAWS FIRST SEASON

Steve Kinser edged Rick Ferkel by 54 points, as the World of Outlaws inaugurated a new era of sprint car racing.

Date	Track	Winner
March 18	Devil's Bowl Speedway, Texas	Jimmy Boyd (Woodruff 21)
April 16	Eldora Speedway, Ohio	Bobby Allen (Allen 1a)
April 30	Eldora Speedway, Ohio	Rick Ferkel (Daugherty 0)
May 21	Eldora Speedway, Ohio	Steve Kinser (Kinser 11)
May 29	Limaland Motor Speedway, Ohio	Rick Ferkel (Daugherty 0)
June 10	Ascot Park, California	Lealand McSpadden (Stanton 75a)
June 10	Calistoga Park, California	Rick Ferkel (Daugherty 0)
June 11	West Capital Speedway, California	Rick Ferkel (Daugherty 0)
June 14	Mercer Raceway, Pennsylvania	Johnny Beaber (Kenemah 3x)
June 16	Skagit Speedway, Washington	Doug Wolfgang (Speedway Motors 4x)
June 17	Skagit Speedway, Washington	Doug Wolfgang (Speedway Motors 4x)
June 24	Lincoln Speedway, Pennsylvania	Steve Smith (Fletcher 66)
July 3	Eldora Speedway, Ohio	Rick Ferkel (Daugherty 0)
July 8	Limaland Motor Speedway, Ohio	Steve Kinser (Kinser 11)
July 15	Missouri State Fairgrounds	Rick Ferkel (Daugherty 0)
July 22	Limaland Motor Speedway, Ohio	Steve Kinser (Kinser 11)
July 29	Lincoln Speedway, Pennsylvania	Steve Smith (Slaybaugh 61)
August 1	Kokomo Speedway, Indiana	Steve Kinser (Kinser 11)
August 3	Eldora Speedway, Ohio	Randy Ford (Ford 10)
August 4	Eldora Speedway, Ohio	Rick Ferkel (Daugherty 0)
August 5	Eldora Speedway, Ohio	Rick Ferkel (Daugherty 0)
August 12	Knoxville Speedway, Iowa	Doug Wolfgang (Speedway Motors 4x)
August 18	Bloomington Speedway, Indiana	Steve Kinser (Kinser 11)
August 22	Warsaw Speedway, Indiana	Bobby Allen (Allen 1a)
August 23	Oakshade Raceway, Ohio	Steve Smith (Fletcher 66)
September 2	Paragon Speedway, Indiana	Steve Kinser (Kinser 11)
September 3	Eldora Speedway, Ohio	Steve Kinser (Kinser 11)
September 9	Colorado National Speedway	Steve Kinser (Kinser 11)
September 16	Devil's Bowl Speedway, Texas	Sammy Swindell (Brown 44)
September 21	Lawton Speedway, Oklahoma	Sammy Swindell (Brown 44)
September 23	Calistoga Fairgrounds, California	Johnny Anderson (Woodruff 21)
September 24	Williams Grove, Pennsylvania	Kramer Williamson (Apple House 41)
September 29	West Capital Speedway, California	Steve Kinser (Kinser 11)
September 30	New York State Fairgrounds	Bentley Warren (Snyder 77)
September 30	New York State Fairgrounds	Jimmy Edwards (Moskat 71)
September 30	West Capital Speedway, California	Steve Kinser (Kinser 11)
October 7	Santa Clara Fairgrounds, California	Steve Kinser (Kinser 11)
October 14	Manzanita Speedway, Arizona	Lealand McSpadden (Bailey Bros. 01)
October 21	Ascot Park, California	Buster Venard (Venard 7)
October 22	Speedway 117, California	Rick Goudy (Morales Bros. 2)
October 29	Eldora Speedway, Ohio	Shane Carson (Nickles Brothers 31)

Duane Carter, Sr.*
Joie Chitwood, Sr.*
Chris Economaki
Ira Hall*
Jim Hurtubise*
Walt James
Roger McCluskey*
Troy Ruttman*
Myron Stevens*
Bob Trostle
Ira Vail*
A.J. Watson
Frank Winkley*

1994
Ralph Capitani
Earl Baltes
Karl Kinser
Fred Offenhauser*
Deb Snyder*
Don Branson*
Jimmy Bryan*
Leo Goossen*
Sig Haugdahl*
Frank Kurtis*
O.D. Lavely*
George "Doc" MacKenzie*
Marshall "Shorty" Pritzbur*
Elbert "Babe" Stapp*
Jimmy Wilburn*

1995
Bill Ambler*
John Ambler*
Bob Sweikert*
Pete Folse*
Pete DePaolo*
Bill Hill
Rick Ferkel
Pat O'"Connor*
Gaylord White*
Frankie Luptow*

Richard "Mitch" Smith*
Wally Meskowski*
Don Smith
Johnny Rutherford
LaVern Nance
Louis Vermeil*

1996
Emil Andres*
Lynn Paxton
Roy Richwine*
Mike Nazaruk*
Bill Pickens*
Russ Clendenen
Rollie Beale
Willie Davis
Mario Andretti
Ted Halibrand*
John Sloan*
Jerry Blundy*
J.W. Hunt*
Tom Bigelow
Paul Weirick*
Johnny Thomson*

1997
Bruce Bromme, Sr.*
Tom Cherry*
Charlie Curryer*
Vern "Flip" Fritch*
Hiram Hillegass*
Joe James*
Leo Krasek*
W. H. "Stubby" Stubblefield*
Dick "Toby" Tobias*
Bobby Unser
Dick Wallen
Travis "Spider" Webb*
Kenny Weld*
Harry "Barney" Wimmer*
Gordon Woolley

John Hererra leads the way in a 1998 World of Outlaws event at Tri-State Speedway. *Randy Jones*

1998
Bobby Allen
Sam Hanks*
Norman "Bubby" Jones
Gary Patterson*
Bill Schindler*
Greg Weld
Dean Thompson
Harry Hartz*
Grant King*
Bob Weikert
Tom Holden*
Ted Johnson
Gene Van Winkle*

1999
Al Gordon*
Ray Lee Goodwin
Eddie Sachs*
Lealand McSpadden
Bob Kinser
Clarence "Hooker" Hood
Johnny White*
LeRoy Van Conett
Russ Garnant*
Steve Stapp
Granvel "Hank" Henry*
Don Basile*
John Sawyer
Fred Loring*
Larry Sullivan*

2000

Al "Cotton" Farmer
Chester "Chet" Gardner*
Earl Halaquist*
Allen Heath*
Bert Emick
L. A. "Les"* and Beryl Ward
Harold Leep
Jimmy Oskie
Joe Saldana
Steve Smith
Tom Marchese*
Bob Russo*
Paul Fromm*
August "Gus" Hoffman*
D. William "Speedy Bill" Smith
Chester "Chet" Wilson*

2001

Emmett "Buzz" Barton
Brad Doty
Bob Hogle
Eddie Leavitt
Albert "Buddy" Taylor*
Davey Brown, Sr.
Bob Estes*
Gary Stanton
Don Martin*
Jack Miller
Dick Sutcliffe
Don Mack

WORLD OF OUTLAWS SEASON CHAMPIONS

1978 Steve Kinser
1979 Steve Kinser
1980 Steve Kinser
1981 Sammy Swindell
1982 Sammy Swindell
1983 Steve Kinser
1984 Steve Kinser
1985 Steve Kinser
1986 Steve Kinser
1987 Steve Kinser
1988 Steve Kinser
1989 Bobby Davis Jr.
1990 Steve Kinser
1991 Steve Kinser
1992 Steve Kinser
1993 Steve Kinser
1994 Steve Kinser
1995 Dave Blaney
1996 Mark Kinser
1997 Sammy Swindell
1998 Steve Kinser
1999 Mark Kinser
2000 Steve Kinser
2001 Danny Lasoski

SEASON CHAMPIONS OF THE ALL STAR CIRCUIT OF CHAMPIONS

1980 Bobby Allen
1981 Lee Osborne
1982 Lee Osborne
1983 Lee Osborne
1984 Fred Linder
1985 Jack Hewitt
1986 Fred Linder
1987 Joe Gaerte
1988 Joe Gaerte
1989 Robbie Stanley
1990 Terry Shepherd
1991 Frankie Kerr
1992 Kevin Huntley
1993 Frankie Kerr & Kevin Huntley (tie)
1994 Frankie Kerr
1995 Dale Blaney
1996 Dale Blaney
1997 Frankie Kerr
1998 Kenny Jacobs
1999 Kenny Jacobs
2000 Kenny Jacobs
2001 Kenny Jacobs

Shock absorbers and other suspension parts are organized for quick access on one team's mule.
Randy Jones

NORTHERN AUTO RACING CLUB (NARC) CHAMPIONS

1960 Fred Hunt
1961 Paul Worden
1962 Marvin Faw
1963 Wally Talbot
1964 Bill Sullivan
1965 Bill Sullivan
1966 Bill Sullivan
1967 Jesse Purssell
1968 Mike McCreary
1969 Leroy VanConett
1970 Leroy VanConett
1971 Billy Anderson
1972 Mike McCreary
1973 Ron Horton
1974 Billy Anderson
1975 Leroy VanConett
1976 Johnny Anderson
1977 Leroy VanConett
1978 Leroy VanConett
1979 Jimmy Boyd
1980 Leroy VanConett
1981 Leroy VanConett
1982 Brent Kaeding
1983 Chuck Gurney
1984 Leroy VanConett
1985 Brent Kaeding
1986 Rick Hirst
1987 Jason McMillen
1988 Brent Kaeding
1989 Brent Kaeding
1990 Tim Green
1991 Brent Kaeding
1992 Tim Green
1993 Brent Kaeding
1994 Brent Kaeding
1995 Brent Kaeding
1996 Brent Kaeding
1997 Brent Kaeding
1998 Brent Kaeding
1999 Brent Kaeding
2000 Brent Kaeding

About the author

Mike O'Leary developed his passion for auto racing very early in life. He covers a broad assortment of motorsports for National Speed Sport News and writes the popular column, "Hoosier Pit Pass," which generally focuses on sprint, midget, and champ car racing. Mike is also a frequent contributor to other motorsports periodicals.

Employed as a program manager by an Indianapolis-based engineering firm, in 1995, Mike retired after 27 years in the Navy and the Navy Reserve. Mike and Sandi O'Leary live in the rolling hills of southern Indiana with a Boston terrier named Boston Louie and four cats.

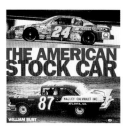

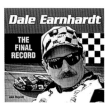